Book 28—Acts

The Early Church

Written by Anne de Graaf

Illustrated by José Pérez Montero

Family Time Bible Stories

Standard Publishing

ACTS—THE EARLY CHURCH

Acts 9—19; James; Galatians; 1 and 2 Thessalonians

About the Letter by James and Paul's Letters to the Galatians and Thessalonians 3

PETER IS THE LEADER
Peter's Ministry 4
A Sheet Full of Animals 6
Peter Visits a Roman Officer 7
Good News for Everyone 9

DON'T GIVE IN
Actions Speak Louder Than Words 11
True Wisdom 13
Peter Escapes From Prison 13
Peter's Friends Forget to Let Him In 14

PAUL'S FIRST MISSIONARY JOURNEY
Paul, the Preacher 15
Choosing to Believe 19

AN URGENT MESSAGE
Children of Promise 19
A Plan for Life 20

PAUL'S SECOND MISSIONARY JOURNEY
Visiting Old and New Churches 21
Paul Arrives in Greece 22
Singing in Prison 24
On the Move 25
Paul in Athens 26
The Church in Corinth 28

A JOYFUL LETTER
An Example to Others 29
Growing Faith 29

PAUL ARRIVES IN EPHESUS
Trouble in Ephesus 30

Old Testament Books 32
New Testament Books 35

About the Letter by James and Paul's Letters to the Galatians and Thessalonians

The early church is the group of people who chose to believe in Jesus after His resurrection. That is what a church is—a group of believers. The early church suffered very much. Jewish religious leaders were against them. Usually the Christians met in secret. They shared everything they owned and took care of each other, while telling others the Good News.

It is to this group that God revealed His plan to offer all people the choice of believing in Jesus. Peter, Paul and the other leaders of the church learned that the forgiveness and hope offered by Jesus is a message for Jews and non-Jews. This is Good News indeed!

James wrote one of the first letters written by leaders of the church to Christians at that time. Many people believe that this is the same James who was Jesus' brother. He went on to become the leader of the Jerusalem church. James wrote about wisdom and making sure our actions match what we say we believe.

During these years of the early church, God worked many miracles through the apostles as they preached and prayed and healed in Jesus' name. Nothing could stop the apostles from talking to people about Jesus, not even prison chains and barred doors. As always though, no amount of miracles could convince those who closed their minds and hearts to the messages of God.

Paul wrote to his friends in Galatia (central Turkey) around A.D. 47. He reminded them that God's gift of forgiveness is free to all who believe. No one can earn it. No one ever deserves it. All we can do is receive it like any gift, and allow God to mold our lives around it.

Paul and the other missionaries traveled from one place to the next, preaching about Jesus and starting churches as they went. The church in Thessalonica is one example where a whole Christian community grew up around what Paul had taught them, despite his short time with them. The seed of the Good News took root. The believers in Thessalonica acted on what they heard Paul teach about the Good News of Jesus.

PETER IS THE LEADER

Peter's Ministry

Acts 9:32-43

As time went by, the Good News of Jesus' resurrection spread throughout the area. More and more people became believers. More and more people shared their faith with others.

Peter went to the towns and villages where groups of believers met. One such place was the town of Lydda, near Joppa. There he found a man named Aeneas. He could not move. For eight years he had not been able to get out of bed. Peter said to him. "Aeneas, Jesus Christ heals you. Get up and make your bed."

Right away, Aeneas was able to get out of bed! And everyone who lived in the area and saw him turned to the Lord.

After Aeneas was healed, a certain woman in nearby Joppa became very sick and died. Her name was Tabitha. Her Greek name was Dorcas, which means "a deer." She was one of the believers in that city. Everything she said and did was good. She was kind to everyone she met, no matter who they were.

When Tabitha died, the disciples in Joppa sent for Peter. "Come to us as quickly as possible," they said. When Peter arrived, he found many women crying for their dead friend. They even showed Peter the clothes she had sewn for other people while she was alive.

When Peter sent everyone out of the room, he knelt and prayed. Then he said, "Tabitha, get up." And she opened her eyes! When she saw Peter, she sat up. Peter gave her his hand and helped her get up. Then he called the other believers. Everyone was filled with wonder and the story spread throughout Joppa. Many people came to believe in Jesus after this. And Peter spent many days in Joppa.

5

A Sheet Full of Animals

Acts 10:1-16

Jesus' teaching was spreading. Although most Jews had turned their backs on it, many risked their very lives and believed. The time had come, though, for more people than just the Jews to hear the good news.

A few times in Jewish history, God had spoken through His prophets and said how there would come from the Jewish people a Light that would save the world. Even Jesus had mentioned that His teaching, although for the Jews at first, would also be offered to those of all races. This was one reason why the religious leaders had hated Him so much. They did not like the idea of not being God's chosen people. Now the time had come for all that to change. God made this clear through two men, Peter and a man named Cornelius.

Cornelius was an army officer from Rome. Even so, he and his family believed in the one God. Cornelius was a man of prayer, and he gave much of his money to help the poor.

One day Cornelius had a vision of an angel who called, "Cornelius!"

"What is it, Lord?"

"God has heard your prayers and noticed your gifts. He remembers you. Now send your men to Joppa to bring back a man named Simon Peter. He is living in a house by the sea." So Cornelius sent three of his most trusted soldiers to Joppa.

The next day, a strange thing happened to Peter. He had gone up to the flat roof of the house to pray. It was about noon and Peter was hungry.

As Peter was praying, he had a vision. He saw Heaven open and a great sheet come down. Inside it were all kinds of animals, reptiles, and birds. A voice told him, "Get up, Peter. You may kill and eat these!"

But Peter said, "Oh no, Lord! I have never eaten anything unholy or unclean." Then the voice told him, "God has made these things clean. Don't call them unholy." This happened three times. Then the sheet was taken back to Heaven.

Peter Visits a Roman Officer

Acts 10:17-48

Peter was confused. "What could this vision mean?" he wondered. Then, as if to answer his question, that very same moment, the three men sent by Cornelius arrived at the gate.

God's Holy Spirit told Peter, "Get up now and go downstairs. Three men are looking for you. Don't worry, I have sent them."

Peter went downstairs and heard from the three men how Cornelius had been told by an angel to send for Peter. So the next day he set out with some of the brothers from Joppa. When he arrived at the house, all of Cornelius' friends and family were there. Cornelius fell at Peter's feet to worship him. But Peter said, "Get up. I'm a

7

8

man, just like you are."

Peter looked around the room. It was filled with people who were not Jews. He said, "You know yourselves that it is against the Jewish law for me to visit you. Yet God has shown me that I should not call any man unholy or unclean. That's why I'm here. Now please tell me why you sent for me."

Then Cornelius told Peter what the angel had said to him during the vision. Peter nodded; it was becoming very clear to him.

"God does not play favorites. I see that now. Anyone who worships God and does what is right is welcomed by Him. The peace He sent to the Jews through Jesus is for any who believe. Even the prophets have written that, through Jesus, everyone who believes in Him will be forgiven."

Suddenly, the Holy Spirit came down on all those who were listening to Peter. The brothers from Joppa heard them speaking in different languages and praising God.

Everyone was amazed! Peter said, "Can anyone keep these people from being baptized with water? They have received the Holy Spirit the same way we did." Then Peter ordered that the people be baptized in the name of Jesus Christ.

Good News for Everyone

Acts 11:1-26

Word quickly reached the other apostles that Gentiles had received the word of God. Some thought Peter had broken Jewish law. As soon as Peter came back to Jerusalem, they questioned him.

"You broke the law," the apostles said.

Then Peter explained about his vision, and about the angel who had visited Cornelius. "The Spirit told me to go with the men Cornelius had sent," explained Peter.

Then Peter told how God's Spirit had come to the non-Jews who were in Cornelius' house. "If God gave them the same gift He gave us who believed in the Lord Jesus Christ, who was I to stand in God's way?"

When the other apostles heard this, they quieted down and praised God. "Well then," they said. "God has also given to the Gentiles the way that leads to life."

Meanwhile, believers living outside Jerusalem were also preaching about Jesus. A few even told the Greeks about Jesus. Many believed and turned to the Lord.

When news of this reached Jerusalem, they sent Barnabas to see what was happening. He went to Antioch and his heart was full of joy when he saw how many people were coming to Jesus.

Barnabas talked to the people of Antioch, and even more people became disciples. Then he went to Tarsus to look for Saul. Barnabas brought Saul back to Antioch. They stayed there together, teaching many people, Jews and non-Jews, who had chosen to follow Jesus. It was in Antioch that the believers were, for the first time, called "Christians."

DON'T GIVE IN

Actions Speak Louder Than Words

James 1:1—3:12

Any time is an exciting one for the followers of Jesus. But these early years of the church were particularly exciting. The Jews had grown more and more bound by the rules the religious leaders had made them follow. When they chose to believe in Jesus, rules were no longer the most important part of their belief. Following Jesus is so simple, even a child can understand. And that is exactly what Jesus wants.

But the apostles did not want the new followers of Jesus to make the mistake of thinking they could live any way they chose. Saying, "I believe in Jesus" is the best of all possible starts. But the right actions must follow.

One of the church leaders at this time was a man named James. James warned that words were not enough. Following Jesus takes faith. And faith is something that only grows stronger when it is practiced.

James wrote, "Ask in faith without any doubting. The one who doubts is like the surf of the sea, driven and tossed by the wind."

"If anyone is a hearer of the Word and not a doer, he is like a man who looks at his face in a mirror. When he walks away, he forgets right away what he looks like."

"Control your tongue. Visit orphans and widows. Don't let the world cause you to sin. Don't show favor to the rich. Remember that God chose the poor of this world to be rich in faith."

"If someone needs clothing and food and you say, 'Go in peace,' but don't give them what is needed, what use is that? Faith without works is useless."

11

True Wisdom

James 3:13—5:20

James also taught about wisdom. He said that the wisdom of those who follow Jesus is different than the wisdom of the world. In the world, those who are well-educated, or rich and powerful are usually considered wise. But the type of wisdom James taught is a gift from God. In God's eyes, a man is wise when he puts aside his own desires and helps others. This wisdom guides a person's every word and action.

"Let those of you who are wise and understanding show it in the way you act. The wisdom from above is pure, peaceful, easy to please. It is fair and honest, ready to help others."

How do we receive God's wisdom? By praying for it. God is generous. He enjoys giving to us. Prayer is also the way of avoiding the trouble and danger we sometimes get ourselves into when we think we have all the answers.

Patience and prayer—those are the two words of wisdom James shared with his fellow-Christians. James said, "When in trouble, ask God for help. When joyful, thank God."

Peter Escapes From Prison

Acts 12:1-10

More and more people listened to leaders like James, even though doing so was dangerous.

Because the Jewish leaders had begun to hunt Jesus' followers and put them in prison, many of them had left Jerusalem. Wherever they went, they told others about Jesus.

King Herod began to do terrible things to the followers of Jesus. He put some of the leaders in jail. Then he had James, the brother of John, killed.

The death of James made the Jewish religious leaders very happy. When Herod saw he had pleased them, he searched for and arrested Peter. Herod threw him in prison and ordered sixteen soldiers to guard him. "After the Passover we will put him on trial," King Herod thought. But God had other plans. While Peter was in prison, the church kept praying for him.

The night before Peter was due to go on trial, he was sleeping between two soldiers, bound to them with chains.

Peter's Friends Forget to Let Him In

Acts 12:11-24

Peter shook his head. It had all seemed like a dream, yet there he was, outside the prison. "Now I know for sure that the Lord has sent His angel to rescue me," he thought.

When he realized this, he made his way to the house of Mary, the mother of John Mark. A group of Christians were having a prayer meeting there.

When Peter knocked at the door, a servant named Rhoda answered. When she heard his voice, she was so happy that she ran to the others and said,

"Peter! It's Peter outside!" She was so excited she had forgotten to let him in!

The others said, "You're out of your mind!" But Rhoda knew it was true. Finally someone said, "Well, maybe it was his angel."

All this time, Peter had been knocking on the door. Finally someone opened the door. It really was Peter! The Christians were so excited, everyone started to talk at once.

Peter held up his hand for silence. Then he told how the Lord had let him out of prison. "Now be sure and tell the others what happened," he said. Then he went to another place.

The next morning, when the soldiers found Peter had escaped, they knew they were in trouble. They turned the prison upside down, trying to find Peter. King Herod was so angry, he ordered that the guards be killed.

There were also guards at the door.

Suddenly, an angel of the Lord filled the prison cell with light. He touched Peter and said, "Get up quickly." As Peter stood up, the chains fell off of him! "Put on your sandals and coat, then follow me!" said the angel.

Peter did as he was told, but he did not believe it was real. "I must be dreaming," he thought. One by one, they passed the guards, yet no one even looked at Peter! The gates into the city opened by themselves and Peter stepped out onto the street. Then the angel left him.

PAUL'S FIRST MISSIONARY JOURNEY

Paul, the Preacher

Acts 12:24—13:52

After Herod's death, the Good News about Jesus spread to more and more places.

The Holy Spirit spoke to the leaders of the church at Antioch. "I have chosen Barnabas and Saul to do a special work," He told them.

The men all prayed and worshiped the Lord. Then they laid their hands on Barnabas and Saul and sent them out.

These two men, along with John Mark, a young relative of Barnabas, were the first missionaries. They traveled from area to area, spreading the news about Jesus. Sometimes they ran into enemies who tried to stop them. One of these was a man named Elymas, a magician and false prophet.

One day, as Saul and Barnabas were speaking to a governor named Sergius

Paulus, Elymas tried to stop them. Saul, who was now called Paul, told him, "You son of the devil! You are full of lies. Now you'll be blind for a while." Then everything became dark for Elymas. He went around trying to find someone to lead him by the hand. When the governor saw this, he believed. He was amazed at the things Paul and Barnabas told him

At Perga, John Mark left Paul and Barnabas to go back to Jerusalem. Paul and Barnabas went on to another town. On the Sabbath they visited the synagogue. When the people saw them, they said, "It's not often we have visitors from Jerusalem. If you have something encouraging to say to us, please speak."

And so Paul preached to the people about Jesus, the Messiah, the One sent by God to save His people. As Paul and Barnabas were leaving, the people asked them to come back the next Sabbath to tell them more.

A week later they came to preach again, and the crowds were even larger. Almost everyone in the city had come to hear Paul preach.

The Jewish leaders did not like this. They were jealous of Paul and Barnabas. So they began to say insulting things and argued against what Paul and Barnabas were saying. Paul explained that God had sent them to preach the Good News about Jesus to the Jews first. "But now, since you choose not to listen, we are preaching to the Gentiles. This is what the Lord has told us to do. The gospel is for everyone!"

When the people understood that Jesus' promises were for Jews and Gentiles, the Gentiles were happy. But their enemies decided Paul had to be stopped, no matter what the cost. They started trouble against Paul and Barnabas and drove them out of the area.

So Paul and Barnabas left, looking for places where they were more welcome. But the followers who were left behind were filled with joy and with the Holy Spirit.

Choosing to Believe

Acts 14:1-22

As Paul and Barnabas went from city to city, teaching about Jesus, they made both friends and enemies. Usually their enemies were fellow Jews. They either did not believe the Gentiles could be chosen by God, or they were simply jealous of how popular Paul and Barnabas were.

In one place, God gave Paul and Barnabas many signs and wonders so the people would know He had sent them. Yet many believed the religious leaders who said Paul and Barnabas could not be trusted. Some even tried to kill the apostles with stones.

Paul and Barnabas went to the city of Lystra. There they met a man who had never walked. Paul saw that the man believed God could heal him. So Paul said, "Stand up!" The man jumped up and began to walk!

When the crowds saw this, they said, "These are not men, but gods! The gods have come down to walk with us!" Some people wanted to offer sacrifices to Paul and Barnabas.

When the men saw what was happening, they ran through the crowd shouting, "No! No! Why are you doing this? We are men just like you are. We have come to bring you the Good News about Jesus. We want you to turn away from worthless things and turn to the true living God."

Later, enemies from other cities came and convinced some people to turn against Paul. They threw stones at Paul and left him for dead. But Paul was not dead. He got up and went back to the city. The next day he and Barnabas went to a new city.

AN URGENT MESSAGE
Children of Promise

Galatians 1:1—4:31

The region where Paul and Barnabas went on their first missionary journey was called Galatia. Now it is called Central Turkey. The two men went back and forth, teaching as they went. Wherever they went there always seemed to be some troublemakers.

Paul kept track of the Christians in each city by writing letters to them. One of the first letters Paul wrote was to the Galatian Christians.

Paul wrote that they should be careful not to listen to people who twist God's Word. "I'm amazed at you. You are already turning away and believing a different message."

Paul reminded them that God had singled him out to be an apostle, and that his message was from God. He had preached the Good News about Jesus that God had given him.

He warned the Galatians that they are not saved because they keep the Jewish law but because they have accepted Jesus as their Savior. The law was given to show the wrong things people do. But when Jesus came, the law was no longer needed. Now people are to live by faith in Jesus.

A Plan for Life

Galatians 5:1—6:18

Paul was angry that some of the new Christians believed those who were trying to undo God's good work.

He warned that people can only follow God's plan for their lives if they let the Holy Spirit guide them. Once they're living the way God wants them to, people will become like a tree, bearing the fruit of the Spirit. Paul meant something very special when he wrote this.

How do you know a pear tree from an apple tree? By the fruit. How can you know when people are led by the Spirit? By their actions. People's actions are the fruit of their lives.

"If people live lives that show love, joy, peace, patience, kindness, goodness, faithfulness, gentleness, and self-control, they are allowing God's Spirit to lead them."

Near the end of his letter, Paul wrote, "Let us not become tired of doing good. In time we will receive our reward in Heaven. Don't give up!"

PAUL'S SECOND MISSIONARY JOURNEY

Visiting Old and New Churches

Acts 15:1—16:5

About ten years had passed since God had shown Peter that His forgiveness was for Gentiles as well as for Jews. At that time, Peter and the other apostles had agreed that this was God's will. But some churches were still fighting about this.

Paul had been teaching both Jews and Gentiles. Now he was in trouble with those who believed that everyone who wanted to become a Christian must first become a Jew.

Paul and Barnabas went to Jerusalem to talk to the apostles and elders. There was a long debate. Peter repeated what had happened to him, and Paul and Barnabas told all about the signs and wonders God had done through them among the Gentiles.

When they were finished, James, the brother of Jesus, said, "It is my judgment that we shouldn't bother those who are turning to God from among the Gentiles." The apostles sent word out to all the churches that no one had to become a Jew before accepting Jesus.

After this, Paul suggested to Barnabas that they visit all the towns

21

where they had preached about Jesus. "Let's see how the believers are doing," he said.

Barnabas wanted to take John Mark, but Paul did not agree. John Mark had left them before and might do it again. So Barnabas took John Mark with him, while Paul chose a man named Silas. They set sail for the island of Cyprus.

This was Paul's second missionary journey. He and Silas covered most of the same ground Paul had during the first journey.

In Lystra, Paul and Silas met a young disciple named Timothy. His mother was Jewish, but his father was a Greek. All the Christians in the area had good things to say about Timothy. Paul asked Timothy if he would like to come with him and Silas. Timothy said yes.

In town after town they passed on the news about what had happened in Jerusalem. "You don't need to become Jews before Jesus will forgive you! He'll accept you no matter where you come from!" Every day more and more people came to believe in Jesus.

Paul Arrives in Greece

Acts 16:6-24

Paul and Silas were joined by the doctor, Luke, who made careful notes about their trip.

When Paul and his team of missionaries needed to know where to go next, they prayed to God. And God answered their prayers. His Spirit made it clear where the team should go or not go.

Paul, Timothy, Luke, and Silas had passed through Galatia. "Where to next?" they prayed. The Holy Spirit showed them they should not go toward Asia. He also kept them from going in a second direction as well.

One night, Paul had a vision. He saw a man from Macedonia, a land across the sea. "Come over and help us!" begged the man. The apostles knew God was calling them to preach there. They put out to sea and crossed without any problems.

Philippi was the main city of that region. There were people from all nations here. On the Sabbath, Paul and his group decided to go outside the city gate to a riverside to pray.

There they found a group of women, and Paul began to talk to them. One of the women was named Lydia. She worshiped the true God. The Lord opened her mind to pay attention to Paul. She and the people in her house were baptized. Then she invited Paul and the others to stay at her house.

Another day, as they were going to pray, Paul and Silas met a slave girl who could tell fortunes because she had an evil spirit in her. Her masters made money from this. She followed the men, shouting, "These men are servants of the most High God! They can tell you how to be saved!"

She did this several days. Finally, Paul was bothered so much by this that he commanded the evil spirit to come out of the girl. And it came out!

When her masters saw they could no longer make money with her, they grabbed Paul and Silas and dragged them to the Roman officials. They lied, calling them traitors to Rome. Then an angry mob made sure Paul and Silas were beaten and thrown into prison. Paul and Silas had their feet fastened between large blocks of wood.

Singing in the Prison

Acts 16:25-40

Paul and Silas could barely see each other in the dark. Their backs ached from the beating the guards had given them. It seemed a hopeless time for the two missionaries.

But Paul and Silas did not give up. In fact, they counted it an honor to suffer for Jesus. So what did these two men do? They prayed and sang praises to God!

About midnight, they were singing and praying to God. The other prisoners were listening. Suddenly, a

great earthquake shook the prison from floor to ceiling! The prison doors swung open and everyone's chains fell off.

When the jailer awoke and saw the doors open, he drew his sword and was about to kill himself. He was sure the prisoners had escaped and knew he would be put to death for this. But Paul cried out, "Don't hurt yourself! We're all here!"

The jailer called for a light, and ran inside the prison. Shaking with fear, he fell on his knees before Paul and Silas. Then he brought them out of the prison and asked, "Men, what must I do to be saved?"

The men said, "Believe on the Lord Jesus and you will be saved—you and all those in your house."

Paul and Silas told the jailer and his family the Good News about Jesus. The jailer washed their wounds, then he and all his people were baptized. After this, he took Paul and Silas home with him and gave them food.

The next morning, the judge looked for Paul and Silas to tell them they could go free. He wanted no more trouble. But Paul said, "We are Roman citizens and deserve a fair trial. We will not leave secretly!"

When the judge heard this, he begged Paul and Silas to leave, so he would not get in trouble for arresting Roman citizens. Then the men went back to Lydia's house and said good-bye to the others and left.

On the Move

Acts 17:1-15

Paul and Silas continued to travel until they reached the city of Thessalonica, in northern Greece. There they preached not only to the Jews, but also to the Greeks who had chosen to believe in the one true God. Many of the Greeks joined the group of Christians.

When the Jews saw this, they were jealous. They formed a mob and started a riot. Soon the city was in an uproar! The mob went to find Paul and Silas but they could not find them.

The Christians knew Paul and Silas were in big trouble and did not want anything worse to happen. So, that night the Christians sent Paul and Silas to Berea. There they went to the Jewish synagogue. These Jews were better than the ones of Thessalonica. They wanted to hear what the men had to say. As Paul or Silas talked about how Jesus had come and done the things the prophets said He would, the Jews checked in their Scriptures. Many of the Jews and Greeks believed!

When the Jews of Thessalonica heard where Paul had gone, they came to Berea to cause trouble. The

Christians sent Paul to Athens to protect him. Silas and Timothy stayed at Berea. Then Paul sent a message back to them telling them to come as soon as possible.

Paul in Athens

Acts 17:16-34

Athens was a very important Greek city. It was over one thousand years old. While Paul waited for Timothy and Silas, he walked around the city. He noticed the temples and statues built to the many gods the Greeks worshiped. He even saw one "To the God Who Is Not Known." Paul felt sad that these people did not know the only true God.

In the synagogue, Paul talked with the Jews and the Greeks who worshiped the true God. He also talked with people in the marketplace.

The Greeks took him to a public place so they could hear more. They were always interested in new ideas. They liked nothing better than to argue about something.

Paul told the Greeks, "You are willing to worship any god. You even worship the unknown God so you won't miss one. You don't know who He is, but you worship Him anyway.

"Well, let me tell you, this is the Lord of Heaven and earth. He gives life and breath to all. God wants people to look for Him, and He is not far from any one of us. We live in Him, walk in Him, and are in Him!"

But as Paul went on to talk about how God had raised Jesus from the dead, some of the Greeks laughed at him. "That's crazy!" they said. They didn't want to hear any more. So Paul left them, but some of the people believed Paul and joined him.

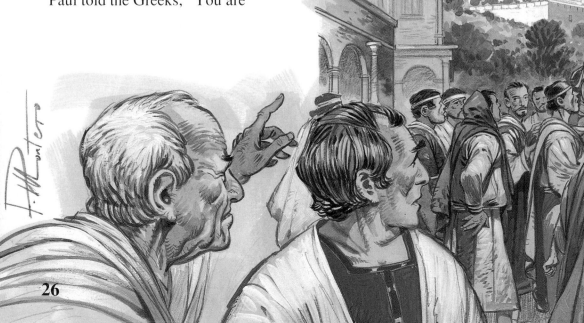

The Church in Corinth

Acts 18:1-17

When Paul left Athens, he went to Corinth, a city famous for the many wicked people who lived there.

Paul found a Jewish couple named Aquila and Priscilla. They were tentmakers just as Paul was. Paul stayed with them and worked with them.

Every Sabbath Paul went to the synagogue to try to persuade the Jews and Greeks that they should believe in Jesus.

When Silas and Timothy joined Paul in Corinth, he was able to spend more time preaching. But the Jews did not want to accept Paul's teaching and some said bad things about him. So Paul turned his back on them and said, "It's your choice whether to believe or not. From now on I'll go to the Gentiles."

In spite of the way these Jews had treated Paul, there were many people in Corinth who wanted to know more about Jesus. One was a Jewish leader named Crispus. He was the ruler of a synagogue. He and all his family became believers.

To encourage Paul, the Lord said to him in a vision, "Don't be afraid, and don't give up. I am with you. No one will hurt you because I have many people in this city."

So Paul settled in Corinth for a year and a half. During this time many chose to believe in Jesus and were baptized. But some of the Jews took Paul to court saying that he was teaching against their law.

The Roman judge told the Jews to stop their complaining. "If this was about a crime, I might agree with you. But you want to cause trouble over a few words and names. Settle this yourselves. I don't want to judge over such things." Then he made them leave.

A JOYFUL LETTER
An Example to Others

1 Thessalonians 1:1—5:28

Paul never forgot about the friends he made during his travels. While Paul was in Corinth he had his hands full with both friends and enemies. Still, he was always praying for and wondering about the churches he had left behind.

Paul sent Timothy from Athens to the believers in Thessalonica. "Go check on the new believers there. Help them and teach them, then let me know how they are doing," Paul said to Timothy.

Paul had only been able to spend a few days in Thessalonica in northern Greece. He had to sneak out so he wouldn't get hurt. He knew other believers may have been hurt after he left. He was anxious to find out from Timothy if the church there was still trying to live as Jesus wanted them to live.

When Timothy returned to Corinth, he told Paul about the strong faith of the Christians in Thessalonica. Paul was overjoyed! Right away he wrote them a letter, encouraging and praising his dear friends.

"Timothy brought us the good news of your faith and love. You are an example to other believers. Keep praying and doing what is good for each other. May the grace of our Lord Jesus Christ be with you."

Growing Faith

2 Thessalonians 1:1—3:18

Paul wrote the Thessalonians another letter. "We always thank God for you.

29

Your faith is growing more and more. You have suffered many troubles, but you still have a strong faith in Jesus. We tell the other churches about you."

Paul encouraged the believers to be strong and to continue believing what he had taught them. "And pray that Jesus' teachings will spread quickly."

Paul reminded the Thessalonians that it is important to work for a living. "We hear that some of you think you don't need to work for a living. You should work quietly and earn your way, not living off the work of others."

PAUL ARRIVES IN EPHESUS
Trouble in Ephesus

Acts 19:8-12, 23-41

After staying in Corinth, Paul traveled to Ephesus. This was across the sea again, back in what is today called western Turkey. Ephesus was a big city with people coming and going. It was a good place to teach the people about following Jesus.

"The Way" is what the Christians called everything that had to do with following Jesus. Believers taught others about the Way. It was probably called this because Jesus had said, "I am the way, the truth and the life. No one comes to the Father, but through me."

Paul spent at least two years in Ephesus talking with people every day about following Jesus. Because of Paul's teaching, every person in that country heard about Jesus. God also

used Paul to do many special miracles.

Before Paul left Ephesus, serious trouble broke out for the Christians. One of the most important false gods in Ephesus was Artemis. Many people worshiped her. A man who made silver statues of Artemis became very angry when he realized Paul had convinced so many people not to worship the false gods.

"That Paul will put all us silversmiths out of business!" he complained. He got enough people upset that a riot broke out. Paul and some of the other believers were in great danger! Men were shouting and the whole city became confused.

Gaius and Aristarchus, two men traveling with Paul, were grabbed and taken into the meeting place. Paul wanted to talk to the crowd, but his friends would not let him. They were afraid the crowd would kill Paul. Some of the people were shouting one thing, some another. Most of the people did not even know why they were there.

Finally, though,

an official calmed the crowd. "Quiet! If you men have a problem with someone, argue in court. Now, go home!"

Jesus' Good News was spreading to people everywhere.

Old Testament

Book 1   **Genesis—In the Beginning**
Genesis 1—22

Book 2   **Israel—Brother Against Brother**
Genesis 23—41

Book 3   **Egypt—The Years from Joseph to Moses**
Genesis 41—50; Exodus 1—11

Book 4   **Exodus—Moses Leads the People**
Exodus 12—40; Deuteronomy 1; Leviticus

Book 5   **Wandering—The Promised Land**
Numbers; Deuteronomy; Joshua 1—4

Book 6   **Canaan—Soldiers of the Lord**
Joshua 5—24; Judges

Book 7   **Faithfulness—Ruth, Job and Hannah**
Ruth; Job; 1 Samuel 1, 2

Book 8   **Samuel—Friends and Enemies**
1 Samuel 2—20

Book 9   **David—From Outlaw to King**
1 Samuel 21—31; Psalms 52, 59, 34, 142, 57, 23, 60; 2 Samuel 1—10;
1 Chronicles 11, 12, 21—22; 2 Chronicles 3

Book 10   **Disobedience—The Fall of David**
2 Samuel 11—24; Psalms 32, 51, 3, 63, 18;
1 Kings 2; 1 Chronicles 11, 12, 21—22; 2 Chronicles 3

Book 11   **Solomon—True Wisdom**
1 Kings 1—4, 6—12; 1Chronicles 22, 28, 29; 2 Chronicles 1—11;
Psalm 72; Proverbs; Song of Solomon; Ecclesiastes

Book 12   **Elijah—Working Wonders**
1 Kings 13—19, 21, 22; 2 Kings 1, 2, 9, 17; 2 Chronicles 12—14, 17—20

Book 13   **Warnings—Elisha and Isaiah**
2 Kings 2, 4—9, 11, 13, 14; 2 Chronicles 21, 22, 25; 1 Kings 19; Isaiah 28—31; Amos

Book 14   **Prophets—Micah, Joel, Jonah and Isaiah**
Hosea; Isaiah 1—9, 36—66; Micah; Joel; Jonah; 2 Kings 15—20; 2 Chronicles 26—32; Psalm 46

Book 15 Kings—Israel and Judah

2 Kings 21—24; 2 Chronicles 33—36; Nahum; Zephaniah;

Jeremiah 1, 2, 11—20, 26—28, 35, 36, 45; Habakkuk; Psalm 73; Ezekiel 1—18

Book 16 Slavery—Daniel In Babylon

2 Kings 24, 25; 2 Chronicles 36; Jeremiah 24, 30, 31, 37—40, 46—52; Ezekiel 24—32;

Isaiah 13—24, 40—43; Psalm 137; Lamentations; Obadiah; Daniel

Book 17 Freed—The New Jerusalem

Ezekiel 33—37, 40—48; Jeremiah 42—44; Isaiah 44—48; Ezra 1—4;

Chronicles 2, 36; Nehemiah 7; Esther

Book 18 Reform—The Last Prophets

Nehemiah 1—10, 12, 13; Ezra 4—10; Haggai; Zechariah; Malachi; Isaiah 56—66